BIBLE TRIVIA FOR KIDS

AGES 8-12

124 New Testament Bible Trivia Questions and Answers

New Testament Bible Trivia Questions

1. In what city was Jesus born?

2. How many books are in the New Testament?

3. What type of insect did John the Baptist eat in the desert?

4. Who were the first apostles called to follow Jesus?

5. How many people did Jesus feed with five loaves of bread and two fish?

6. After Jesus was arrested, which apostle disowned him three times?

7. Who recognized Jesus as the Messiah when he was presented at the Temple as a baby?

8. Who asked Pilate for Jesus' body after the crucifixion?

9. Paul was shipwrecked on what island?

10.   What is the shortest book in the New Testament?

11.   Who is the author of the Book of Revelation?

12.   Matthew was a ____________.

13.   To what city was Saul traveling when he encountered a great and blinding light?

14.   Who was the first person to come upon the injured man in the parable of the Good Samaritan?

15.   Finish this verse. "In every battle you will need faith as your _______ to stop the fiery arrows aimed at you by Satan."

16.   Whose example does Paul say Christians should follow in Chapter 5 of Ephesians?

17.   After Jesus fed 5,000+ people with two fish and five loaves of bread, how many baskets were left over?

18.   What does Paul say may "abound more and more in knowledge and in all judgment?"

19.   What tribe is Paul from?

20.   According to the Beatitudes who will be filled?

21.   What does Simon Peter do for a living before he becomes an apostle?

22.   In the Gospel of Mark, how does the Virgin Mary learn of her pregnancy?

23.   Who is Stephen in Acts of the Apostles?

24.   By what name is Paul of Tarsus known before he begins his missionary activity?

25.   According to Paul's formulation in 1 Corinthians, which is the greatest of the imperishable qualities?

26.   Who is the high priest of Jerusalem who put Jesus on trial?

27.   In the Gospel According to John, which of the apostles doubts Jesus's resurrection until he sees Jesus with his own eyes?

28.   According to the Gospel of Matthew, where does Jesus's first public sermon take place?

29.   How does Judas signal Jesus's identity to the Roman officials?

30.   Who murders John the Baptist?

31.   When Christians observe Palm Sunday, what biblical narrative are they celebrating?

32.   According to the Gospels, what is the unique literary genre Jesus employs to preach his message?

33.   Which Gospel is most concerned with the mystery and identity of the person of Jesus?

34.   Who baptizes Jesus?

35.   Who takes Jesus's body off the cross?

36.   Who is the first apostle to deny Jesus?

37.   Which Gospel is written by a doctor?

38.   What is the common name given to the first four books of the New Testament?

39.   Who wrote most of the books in the New Testament?

40.   Who wrote the Acts of the Apostles?

41.   Which book comes last in the New Testament?

42.   What does the word gospel mean?

43.   Who was the king of Judea at the time of Jesus' birth?

44.   Which gospel records the fewest of the miracles performed by Jesus?

45.   In what water was Jesus baptized?

46.   What miracle did Jesus perform at the marriage in Cana?

47.   Who was the tax collector that climbed up a tree so he could see Jesus?

48.   Which two Old Testament characters appeared with Jesus at the transfiguration?

49.   How did Jesus reveal the one who would betray him?

50.   Where was Jesus crucified?

51.   For how many days did Jesus appear to his disciples after his resurrection?

52.   Who went with Paul on his first missionary journey?

53.	Paul and Silas were imprisoned during the second missionary journey, but in what city did this happen?

54.	During Paul's third missionary journey, roughly for how long did he minister in the school of Tyrannus at Ephesus?

55.	On what island was Paul shipwrecked as he made his way to Rome?

56.	How many churches of Asia Minor were there?

57.	On what island was John when he was given the vision of Revelation?

58.	In the New Jerusalem described in Revelation, what are the twelve gates made from?

59.	Where was Jesus born?

60.	Why did Joseph take Mary and Baby Jesus to Egypt?

61.   Where did Jesus grow up after returning from Egypt?

62.   What was Jesus' first miracle?

63.   As Jesus and His disciples were crossing the Sea of Galilee in a boat, a big storm arose. Jesus rebuked the wind and waves and the storm disappeared. What was Jesus doing when the storm arose?

64.   Jesus miraculously broke just a few loaves of bread and fishes and fed 5000 men, along with women and children. How many loaves and fishes did he start with?

65.   How did Judas identify Jesus as the one to be arrested?

66.   On Good Friday, Jesus was brought before Pontius Pilate for trial. Why did Pontius Pilate condemn Jesus to death?

67. What language was most of the New Testament originally written in?

68. What is the last book of the New Testament?

69. In which Gospel did Jesus say and quote: "Everything is possible for one who believes."?

70. What is John the baptizer's father's name?

71. Who wrote Acts of Apostles?

72. What is the first book of the New Testament?

73. What was the name of first Christian who was stoned to death?

74. For how many days and night was Jesus fasted?

75. Which wood has been used by Noah to build the ark?

76. Where was Jesus born?

77.   How many apostles did Jesus have?

78.   What is the name of the disciple who betrayed Jesus?

79.   How did Jesus die?

80.   Who gave Jesus gifts when he was born?

81.   With what did Jesus feed 5000 people?

82.   Who are the religious leaders who continually tried to trap Jesus with their questions?

83.   What is the name of Jesus' mother?

84.   What did Jesus do for Lazarus?

85.   What job did Jesus' earthly father, Joseph, do?

86.   Who wrote many of the letters to churches in the New Testament?

87.	What is the collective name of the stories Jesus told?

88.	Who wanted to kill Jesus when he was a baby?

89.	What did Simon Peter do for a living?

90.	What happened to Jesus after the resurrection?

91.	What did the Holy Spirit look like when the disciples received it?

92.	Who went on missionary journeys to preach to the Gentiles?

93.	How did Paul escape from Damascus?

94.	What is the last book of the New Testament?

95.	How many apostles did Jesus have?

96.	Which book tells about the visit of the Wise men to baby Jesus?

97.   Who wrote the book of Acts?

98.   How many Gospel books are there?

99.   Who wrote the book of Revelation?

100.   Who said, "Repent, for the Kingdom of Heaven
is at hand"?

101.   How many times did Peter deny Jesus?

102.   Who was shipwrecked in the New Testament?

103.   Which New Testament book talks about Paul's
conversion?

104.   Where did Jesus grow up?

105.   Where was Paul when he went blind?

106.   How many wise and foolish girls were in Jesus'
story?

107.   Who wrote the most books in the New Testament?

108.   Name one book that tells of Jesus' birth?

109.   Who was the governor who tried Jesus?

110.   How many loaves of bread did Jesus use to feed five thousand?

111.   Who said, "Peace, be still"?

112.   Who said, "He is not here; for He is risen"?

113.   Who betrayed Jesus?

114.   Which apostle was a tax collector?

115.   Who lived on locusts and wild honey?

116.   Who was a blind man healed by Jesus?

117.   How many days was Lazarus dead before Jesus brought him back to life?

118.   Who was king of Judea at Jesus' birth?

119.   Who came to Jesus at night?

120.   Which angel appeared to Mary?

121.   What are the names of the Gospel books?

122.   Whom did Jesus call the "Comforter"?
123.   What did the rich young ruler not want to give up?

124.   What disease did Jesus heal ten men of?

ANSWERS

1. Bethlehem
2. 27
3. Locusts
4. Peter and Andrew
5. about 5000 men
6. Peter
7. Simeon
8. Joseph of Arimathea
9. Malta
10. 2 John
11. John
12. Tax collector
13. Damascus
14. Priest
15. Shield
16. Christ's
17. 12
18. Love
19. Benjamin

20.   Those who hunger and thirst for righteousness

21.   He was a fisherman.

22.   From the angel Gabriel

23.   The first Christian martyr

24.   Saul

25.   Love

26.   Caiaphas

27.   Thomas

28.   On the mount

29.   He kisses him.

30.   Herod Antipas

31.   Jesus's entry into Jerusalem before his death

32.   The parable

33.   John

34.   John the Baptizer

35.   Joseph of Arimathea

36.   Peter

37.   Luke

38.   The Gospels

39.   Paul
40.   Luke
41.   Revelation
42.   Good news
43.   Herod the Great
44.   Matthew
45.   River Jordan
46.   Turning water into wine
47.   Zacchaeus
48.   Elijah and Moses
49.   Dipped a piece of bread and passed it to him
50.   Golgotha
51.   40
52.   Barnabas
53.   Philippi
54.   2 years
55.   Malta
56.   Seven
57.   Patmos
58.   Pearl

59.   Bethlehem
60.   To escape from King Herod, who wanted to
   kill Jesus
61.   Nazareth
62.   Turning water into wine
63.   Sleeping
64.   5 loaves and 2 fishes
65.   He kissed Jesus.
66.   The chief priests had persuaded the crowd
   to demand his execution.
67.   Greek
68.   Revelation
69.   Mark
70.   Zacharias
71.   Luke
72.   Mathew
73.   Stephen
74.   40
75.   Gopher
76.   Bethlehem
77.   12

78.   Judas Iscariot

79.   He was crucified.

80.   The wise men

81.   Loaves and fishes

82.   Pharisees

83.   Mary

84.   Raised him from the dead

85.   Carpenter

86.   Paul

87.   Parables

88.   Herod

89.   He was a fisherman.

90.   He ascended into heaven

91.   Tongues of fire

92.   Paul

93.   In a basket down the city wall

94.   Revelation

95.   Twelve

96.   Matthew

97.   Luke

98.   Four

99.   John
100. John the Baptist
101. Three
102. Paul
103. Acts
104. Nazareth
105. On the road to Damascus
106. Five of each or ten altogether
107. Paul
108. Matthew or Luke
109. Pilate
110. Five
111. Jesus
112. An angel
113. Judas
114. Matthew
115. John the Baptist
116. Bartimaeus
117. Four
118. Herod
119. Nicodemus

120. Gabriel

121. Matthew, Mark, Luke and John

122. The Holy Spirit

123. His riches

124. Leprosy

BIBLE TRIVIA
Questions and Answers